P9-CRH-678

Fact Finders®

CAUSE AND EFFECT: AMERICAN INDIAN HISTORY

# *Defending* THE Land

CAUSES AND EFFECTS of Red Cloud's War

BY NADIA HIGGINS

Consultant:
Brett Barker, PhD
Associate Professor of History
University of Wisconsin–Marathon County

CAPSTONE PRESS
a capstone imprint

Fact Finders Books are published by Capstone Press,
1710 Roe Crest Drive, North Mankato, Minnesota 56003
www.capstonepub.com

Copyright © 2015 by Capstone Press, a Capstone imprint. All rights reserved. No part of this publication may be reproduced in whole or in part, or stored in a retrieval system, or transmitted in any form or by any means, electronic, mechanical, photocopying, recording, or otherwise, without written permission of the publisher.

**Library of Congress Cataloging-in-Publication Data**
Higgins, Nadia.
 Defending the land: causes and effects of Red Cloud's War / by Nadia Higgins.
    pages cm.—(Fact finders. Cause and effect: American Indian history)
 Includes bibliographical references and index.
 Summary: "Explains Red Cloud's War, including its chronology, causes, and lasting effects"—Provided by publisher.
 Audience: Grades 4-6.
 ISBN 978-1-4914-2035-5 (library binding)
 ISBN 978-1-4914-2210-6 (paperback)
 ISBN 978-1-4914-2225-0 (ebook PDF)
 1. Red Cloud's War, 1866-1867—Juvenile literature. 2. Red Cloud, 1822–1909—Juvenile literature.
 I. Title.
  E83.866.H55 2015
  978.0049752440092—dc23  [B]                    2014033148

**Editorial Credits**
Catherine Neitge, editor; Bobbie Nuytten, designer; Eric Gohl, media researcher;
Morgan Walters, production specialist

**Source Notes**
Page 7, line 6: Bob Drury and Tom Clavin. *The Heart of Everything That Is: The Untold Story of Red Cloud, an American Legend*. New York: Simon & Schuster, 2013, p. 97.
Page 10, line 9: Ibid., p. 244.
Page 16, line 11: Shannon Smith. "New Perspectives on the Fetterman Fight." WyoHistory.org. 18 Sept. 2014. http://www.wyohistory.org/essays/new-perspectives-fetterman-fight
Page 24, line 7: *Second Annual Report of the Board of Indian Commissioners to the Secretary of the Interior for Submission to the President for the Year 1870*. Washington, D.C.: Government Printing Office, 1871, p. 41. 18 Sept. 2014. https://archive.org/details/annualreportofbo02unitrich

**Photo Credits**
Bridgeman Images: Denver Public Library, Western History Collection/David Frances Barry, cover, © Look and Learn/Private Collection, 15; Corbis: 26; CriaImages.com: Jay Robert Nash Collection, 7, 9, 10, 19; The Granger Collection, NYC: 17; Library of Congress: 5, 21, 23, 25; Newscom: akg-images, 24, EPA/Mike Nelson, 28, Picture History, 12; Wikimedia: U.S. National Archives and Records Administration, 20

Design Elements: Shutterstock

Printed in the Canada.
102014    008478FRS15

# Table of *Contents*

# Famous
# LAKOTA WARRIOR

Red Cloud is a name that has largely been lost to history. But in the late 1800s, that famous name sparked admiration among American Indians and whites alike. Lakota chief Red Cloud once controlled an area of the **Great Plains** that was twice the size of Texas.

Red Cloud saw his empire slowly chipped away by white settlers. In 1866 U.S. forces came to open a road through his best hunting grounds. That was the last straw.

For two years Red Cloud led a war on civilians and soldiers in Wyoming. He gathered an army of Lakota Sioux, Northern Cheyenne, and Arapaho warriors. Red Cloud didn't have the firepower to match his enemy. So he made up for it with planning and **strategy**. For one of the few times in history, Indian forces won a war against the United States.

What caused this unusual war? What happened as a result? Red Cloud's War has been largely forgotten, but its effects are still felt today.

**FAST FACT**

Red Cloud's War was one of the last between the U.S. Army and American Indians. Through the years U.S. troops faced off against native peoples in 1,600 battles and **skirmishes**.

Red Cloud, Lakota warrior and statesman

**Great Plains**—the broad, level land that stretches eastward from the base of the Rocky Mountains for about 400 miles (644 kilometers) in the United States and Canada
**strategy**—a careful plan or method
**skirmish**—a small fight that lasts for a brief time

# What Caused RED CLOUD'S WAR?

By the mid-1860s, Red Cloud believed that the Lakota way of life was in grave danger. Several factors caused the chief alarm.

## Cause #1: Settlers Harm Hunting Grounds

For generations Lakota Indians had survived by hunting buffalo. Lakota bands followed the large hairy animals freely across the Great Plains. By the 1850s, though, hunters noticed that buffalo herds were getting smaller.

White settlers were driving the animals away as they streamed west in search of gold and rich farmland. Whites came with cattle and oxen that ate up the prairie grass. They burned trees for fuel and destroyed watering holes.

In turn, the Plains Indians attacked the settlers' wagon trains. That brought out the U.S. Army to crush the Indian fighters. Government agents also came to make **treaties** with tribal chiefs. These agreements were supposed to bring peace by setting aside Indian land. But as more settlers flocked west, the government broke the treaties.

**FAST FACT**

In the 1840s it might take a full day to ride through a buffalo herd on horseback. Fifty years later the buffalo was almost **extinct**. Today buffalo herds have increased their numbers.

*Swiss painter Karl Bodmer traveled in the West in the 1830s. He captured American Indians hunting buffalo on canvas.*

## Cause #2: The Bozeman Trail

Gold was discovered in 1862 in western Montana. Miners couldn't get there fast enough. The next year John Bozeman and John Jacobs found a shortcut to the gold fields. Using ancient Indian paths, they blazed a route through the heart of Lakota hunting land. The Bozeman Trail broke a treaty promise, but miners poured in anyway. "There are now white people all about me," Red Cloud told a gathering of tribal chiefs and government officials. "I have but a small spot of land left."

**extinct**—no longer living; an extinct animal is one that has died out, with no more of its kind
**treaty**—an official agreement between two or more groups or countries

## Cause #3: A Massacre and an Invasion

Red Cloud was fed up with the white man's destruction, lies, and broken promises. Then, on November 29, 1864, one bloody event took the conflict to a new level.

That morning Colonel John M. Chivington led an attack on a peaceful Cheyenne and Arapaho village along Sand Creek in Colorado. Chief Black Kettle flew an American flag and a white peace flag over his lodge. Even so, Chivington's men slaughtered more than 200 Cheyenne and Arapaho. Most of the dead were women, children, and the elderly.

After that, violence took over. Outraged American Indians stepped up attacks on settlers and Army posts. Warriors from three nations—the Lakota, Cheyenne, and Arapaho—would soon band together into the largest Indian force ever seen.

*The attack by about 675 volunteer soldiers of a peaceful village became known as the Sand Creek Massacre.*

## Cause #4: A Failed Peace Conference

Conflict with the Indians was proving costly for the U.S. government. U.S. leaders hoped to secure the Bozeman Trail by peaceful means. They hosted a peace conference at Fort Laramie, Wyoming, in June 1866.

As the Indian chiefs gathered for talks, Colonel Henry B. Carrington arrived. He was leading a train of 200 wagons and more than 700 soldiers. The troops were on their way to set up forts along the Bozeman Trail.

Red Cloud exploded with anger: "The Great Father sends us presents and wants a new road. But the White Chief already goes with soldiers to steal the road before the Indian says yes or no." As he stalked out, Red Cloud made a promise. "As long as I live I will fight you for the last hunting grounds."

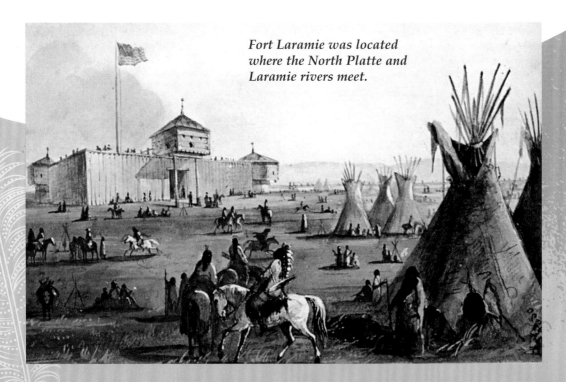

*Fort Laramie was located where the North Platte and Laramie rivers meet.*

# Treaty Making

The United States made about 370 treaties with American Indians from 1778 to 1871. Most of these treaties were doomed from the start by cultural differences, misunderstandings, and foul play.

One problem was finding chiefs who could sign on behalf of their tribes. Many nations, including the Lakota, had several chiefs. Often the government made deals with leaders who had little support from their people. But the leaders were willing to sign treaties favorable to the United States.

In many cases chiefs did not understand what they were signing. Indians had an oral culture and relied on what was said at a treaty meeting. Whites relied on the written language of the treaty. The final written treaty did not always reflect what was said at the negotiations.

Concepts were foreign too. For example, the Lakota idea of land boundaries differed from white culture. Lakota boundaries were more fluid between tribes. Also, Indians often thought they were negotiating passage or use of the land by whites. They did not think they were permanently giving away their right to occupy the land.

Gift giving was an important part of the process. U.S. agents gave out blankets, food, bullets, and other goods to Indians who signed treaties. Chiefs expected to keep some of the goods whether they gave up land or not. Whites, on the other hand, saw the gifts as part of the payment for the land.

# STRATEGY
## and Surprise

Colonel Carrington set out in summer 1866 to establish three forts along the Bozeman Trail in Wyoming's Powder River country. Red Cloud and his warriors carefully watched the Army operation. Red Cloud took note of their weapons, skills, and supplies. He counted their horses and memorized their schedules.

Red Cloud had few guns. He knew that his arrows and clubs were no match for the Army's rifles and cannons. But he held several other advantages. Red Cloud's warriors knew every boulder, ridge, and tree of their territory. They were expert horsemen who could zigzag in and out of hiding places. Red Cloud's warriors also outnumbered Carrington's men by four to one, or more.

*Colonel Henry Carrington*

# Bozeman Trail

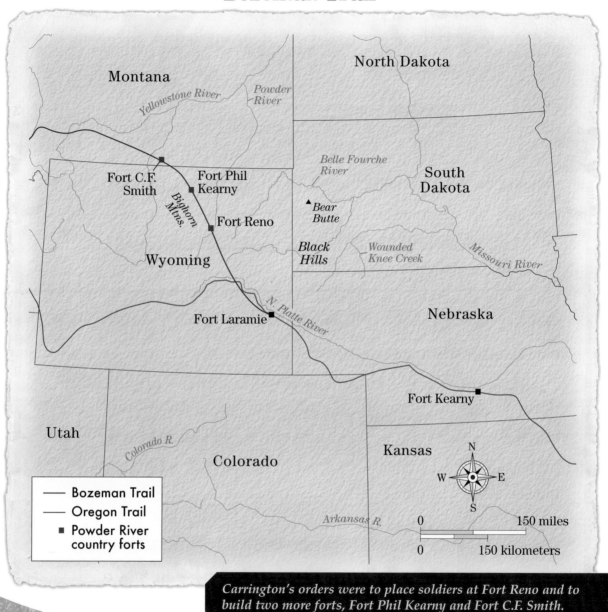

**Montana**

*Yellowstone River*

*Powder River*

**North Dakota**

Fort C.F. Smith

Fort Phil Kearny

*Bighorn Mtns.*

Fort Reno

*Belle Fourche River*

**South Dakota**

▲ *Bear Butte*

*Black Hills*

*Wounded Knee Creek*

*Missouri River*

**Wyoming**

Fort Laramie

*N. Platte River*

**Nebraska**

Fort Kearny

**Utah**

*Colorado R.*

**Colorado**

**Kansas**

N
W E
S

— Bozeman Trail
— Oregon Trail
■ Powder River country forts

*Arkansas R.*

0          150 miles

0          150 kilometers

Carrington's orders were to place soldiers at Fort Reno and to build two more forts, Fort Phil Kearny and Fort C.F. Smith.

## Small, Frequent Attacks

Red Cloud and other Lakota came up with a strategy of small, but steady warfare that would slowly wear down U.S. troops. The Indians would not attack the forts directly. Instead, they would burn, shoot, or frighten any parties that moved beyond the forts. That included soldiers sent to cut wood or hay. Wagons bringing supplies were prime targets, as were traveling settlers and their livestock.

All summer and fall, Red Cloud's men attacked anyone using the Bozeman Trail. The warriors **ambushed** the soldiers almost daily. The Indians seemed to come from nowhere. Just as suddenly, the warriors faded back into the prairie.

Red Cloud kept Carrington's men on edge. Often the Indians attacked after a hard day's work, when the soldiers were most tired. Red Cloud taught his warriors to taunt the soldiers in English. Sometimes warriors dressed in Army uniforms for added insult.

As winter set in, Carrington's men became tired and desperate. Red Cloud faced troubles too. Some of his younger warriors, including Crazy Horse, wanted to move faster. In December 1866 Red Cloud finally ordered a final strike against his enemy.

**ambush**—to attack by surprise from a hidden spot

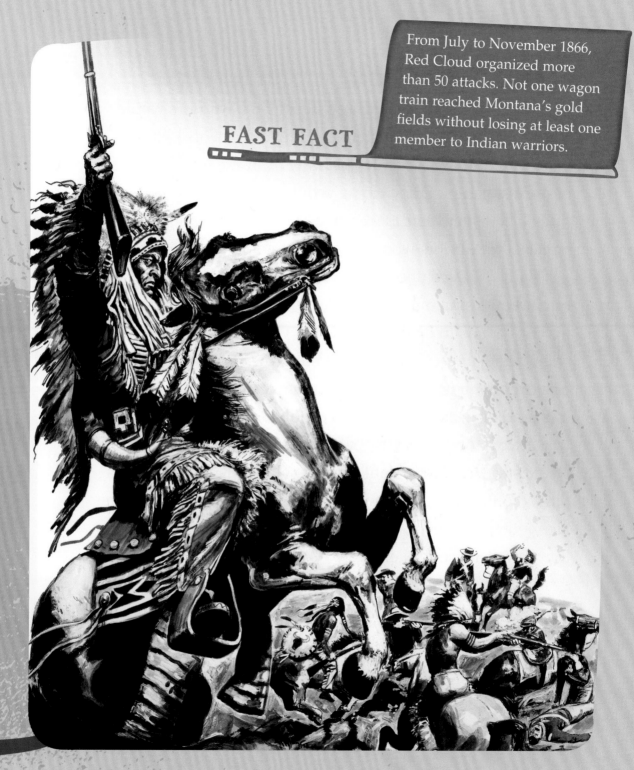

From July to November 1866, Red Cloud organized more than 50 attacks. Not one wagon train reached Montana's gold fields without losing at least one member to Indian warriors.

## The Fetterman Fight

Red Cloud's plan had three steps. First, warriors would attack a group of woodcutters heading out of Fort Phil Kearny. That would draw rescue troops away from the fort. Next, a party of **decoys**, led by Crazy Horse, would **lure** the troops past a ridge. There, between 1,000 and 3,000 warriors would lay in wait. Finally, the warriors would jump out and attack.

Early on December 21, the Indians headed out into the cold, bright day. Using mirrors, smoke, and flags, Red Cloud signaled his commands to his warriors. Soon Captain William Fetterman was leading a rescue party of 80 men toward Crazy Horse's trap. The over-confident Fetterman had earlier boasted, "Give me 80 men and I can ride through the whole Sioux nation."

Crazy Horse and his crew darted in and out of the soldiers' view, waving blankets and yelling insults. As bullets pinged off rocks all around him, Crazy Horse got off his horse. He pretended to tend to the animal. At one point he took in the view as if the soldiers were not even there.

Fetterman was under strict orders not to follow the Indians past the ridge. But the glory-seeking Civil War hero could not resist. He led his men straight into the Indian ambush.

**decoy**—something used to lure a target into a trap
**lure**—to tempt someone to do something or go somewhere

*"Hokahey!"* Charge! With a ferocious roar, the warriors descended on Fetterman's men. The sounds of thundering hooves and hissing arrows filled the air. In 45 minutes the warriors unleashed 40,000 arrows—nearly 1,000 per minute. Not a single member of Fetterman's party survived. It was a stunning defeat for the U.S. Army.

*American Indian deaths are estimated at fewer than 15 in the Fetterman Fight.*

## Unclear Outcomes

That night a blizzard raged across the prairie. Red Cloud's forces retreated for the winter. In spring the Indians renewed their **siege** on the forts.

In late summer 1867, the Indians planned a double attack on Forts C.F. Smith and Phil Kearny. The plan was to ambush hay and woodcutting parties as they headed to their jobs. This time, though, the Indians would face an unwelcome surprise.

In the past the soldiers had used old rifles. The soldiers had to pause to load them from the front. The Indians counted on that pause as their moment to charge. But, unknown to Red Cloud, the soldiers now had new rifles that could fire much faster. The weapons fired eight to 10 shots per minute versus three shots per minute in the older rifles.

The Indians faced rapid, nonstop gunfire in the Hayfield and Wagon Box fights of August 1 and 2. In both cases the warriors retreated without breaking through the soldiers' barricades. Still, the Indians did not consider the battles a defeat. They had captured many Army mules and horses.

**siege**—an attack designed to surround a place and cut it off from supplies or help

The outnumbered soldiers held off the Indians with fast-firing rifles at the Wagon Box Fight on August 2.

## Proud Victory

Meanwhile, the United States was growing ever more weary of Red Cloud's war. Government and business leaders were eager to complete the transcontinental railroad and further open the West.

For months government agents had been sending word to Red Cloud. Would he sit for treaty talks? Each time Red Cloud's answer was the same. He would not sit until the Bozeman Trail was closed.

Finally, in late summer 1868, Red Cloud watched the soldiers leave his last hunting grounds. He and his warriors then burned the Bozeman Trail forts to the ground.

Red Cloud and other Lakota and Arapaho put their Xs on the Treaty of Fort Laramie on November 6, 1868. All of Red Cloud's demands had been met. The Bozeman Trail was gone. Protected Lakota land stretched all the way from South Dakota into Montana and Wyoming. The Lakota's **sacred** Black Hills were promised to them forever.

That day was a proud moment in Red Cloud's life. This proud victory, however, would not last long.

*Peace commissioners, including Civil War General William T. Sherman (third from left, in tent), met with chiefs at Fort Laramie.*

**sacred**—holy

# Fierce Warrior

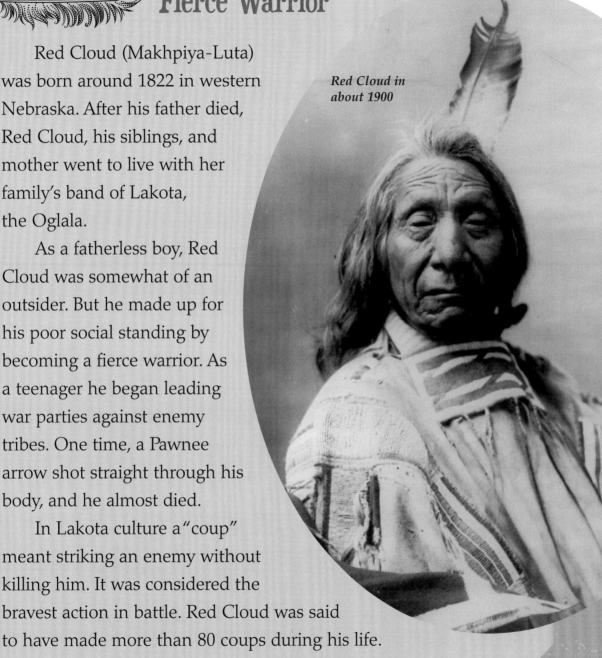

*Red Cloud in about 1900*

Red Cloud (Makhpiya-Luta) was born around 1822 in western Nebraska. After his father died, Red Cloud, his siblings, and mother went to live with her family's band of Lakota, the Oglala.

As a fatherless boy, Red Cloud was somewhat of an outsider. But he made up for his poor social standing by becoming a fierce warrior. As a teenager he began leading war parties against enemy tribes. One time, a Pawnee arrow shot straight through his body, and he almost died.

In Lakota culture a "coup" meant striking an enemy without killing him. It was considered the bravest action in battle. Red Cloud was said to have made more than 80 coups during his life.

# What Effects Did
# RED CLOUD'S WAR HAVE?

Red Cloud's War had surprising—and sometimes devastating—effects for years to come.

## Effect #1: Moving to the Reservation

When Red Cloud signed the Treaty of Fort Laramie, he believed he was protecting the Lakota way of life. The Lakota agreed to live within the Black Hills **reservation**. The Black Hills were Paha Sapa, "The Heart of Everything That Is."

The sacred hills would belong to them forever. But that would not happen.

Over the years the United States seized most of the land that Red Cloud had fought for. This was in direct violation of the Treaty of Fort Laramie. And at the same time, the buffalo was rapidly disappearing from the Great Plains. The huge beasts had provided the Lakota with food, clothing, shelter, and more. Without it, they were nearly powerless to resist the government's policies.

On the Lakota reservation, U.S. agents forced the buffalo hunters to give up their horses and their weapons. People now had to rely on the government for food and other supplies. Today close to 40,000 Lakota live in severe poverty on the Pine Ridge Reservation in South Dakota.

*An Oglala Lakota girl and her puppy in 1891 South Dakota*

**reservation**—an area of land set aside by the government for American Indians; in Canada reservations are called reserves

## Effect #2: From Warrior to Diplomat

Red Cloud felt tricked by the Treaty of Fort Laramie, but he would never go to war again. Instead, he fought for Lakota causes as a **diplomat**. In 1870 he took his first of several trips to Washington, D.C. There he twice met with President Ulysses S. Grant. In the nation's capital Red Cloud experienced the noise and bustle of the city. He saw huge supplies of U.S. weapons.

"The white children have surrounded me and have left me nothing but an island. When we first had this land we were strong. Now we are melting like snow on the hillside, while you are growing like spring grass," he remarked.

*Red Cloud led a group to meet with President Rutherford B. Hayes in 1880. They are (from left) Red Dog, Little Wound, Red Cloud, American Horse, and Red Shirt. Interpreter John Bridgeman stands behind.*

Eventually, Red Cloud lived in a wooden house and became a Christian. Some Lakota chiefs disapproved of him for taking on the white man's ways. But Red Cloud knew that he and his people had to adapt. They had no choice. Red Cloud died in 1909 at Pine Ridge Reservation. He was 88 years old.

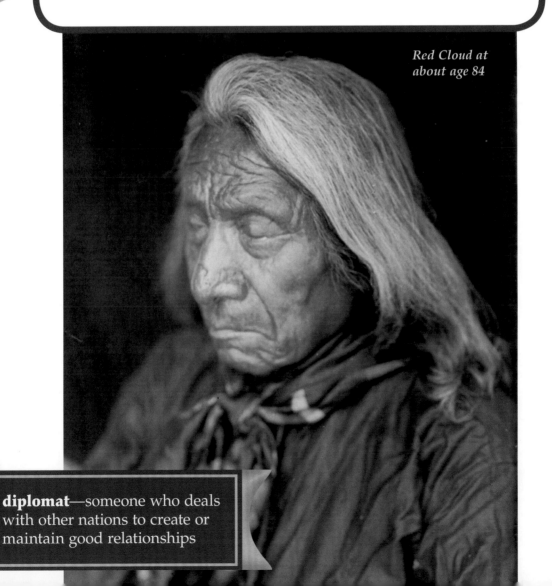

*Red Cloud at about age 84*

**diplomat**—someone who deals with other nations to create or maintain good relationships

# Effect #3: The Struggle for the Black Hills Continues

In the mid-1870s the Treaty of Fort Laramie was broken. Gold had been discovered in the Black Hills. Once again miners were streaming into Lakota land. That sparked the Battle of the Little Bighorn on June 25, 1876. Chief Sitting Bull and his warriors enjoyed a brief victory on the Montana prairie. Red Cloud was not among them. He did not believe the Indians could survive a war against the white man.

After that, the United States was even more determined to seize the Black Hills. U.S. agents presented Red Cloud and other chiefs with an agreement in September 1876 that surrendered the Black Hills. If the chiefs didn't sign it, they would be punished, food would be withheld, and their people would starve. Red Cloud and the others put their Xs on the document.

*Miners search for gold in Deadwood, near the Black Hills, in 1876*

In 1980 the U.S. Supreme Court ordered the government to pay for land it took from the Lakota 100 years earlier. The government was ordered to pay $106 million to Lakota tribes. That is the amount it owed in 1877 plus interest.

Native leaders have refused to claim the funds, which have grown to more than $570 million. They say the sacred Black Hills are still not for sale.

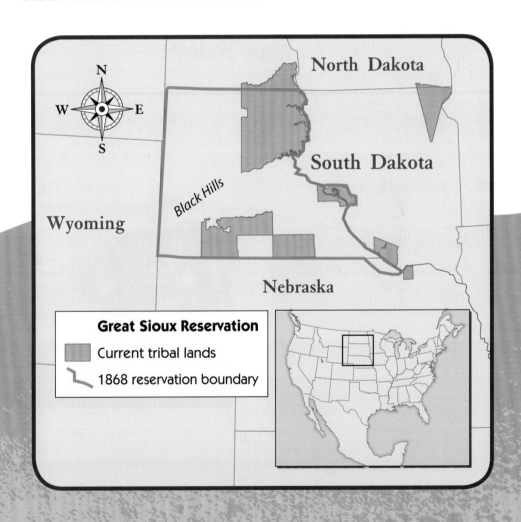

North Dakota

South Dakota

Black Hills

Wyoming

Nebraska

**Great Sioux Reservation**

Current tribal lands

1868 reservation boundary

## Cause and Effect

Red Cloud's War was one of the Lakota's greatest victories. Lakota leaders signed a treaty that they thought would protect their land forever. But time and again, the U.S. government broke the Treaty of Fort Laramie. U.S. policies on reservations almost destroyed the Lakota's culture. They continue to recover today.

# Lakota Today

Reservations dealt a devastating blow to the Lakota culture. Their tribal governments were broken up. Religious practices were outlawed. Lakota children were sent away to boarding schools, where speaking the Lakota language was banned.

*Pine Ridge Reservation powwow dancers*

About 70,000 Lakota remain today. Most of them live on five reservations in North and South Dakota. They are among the poorest areas of the United States.

Even so, the Lakota are enjoying a cultural renewal. At powwows, they gather to celebrate traditional ceremonies, stories, arts, and games. Tribal leaders are making special efforts to preserve Lakota language and history. The Lakota are finding new ways to survive within American culture.

# TIMELINE

**1840**

**1850**

**1860**

**1870**

**1900**

**1980**

**1843:**
Waves of white settlers begin crossing the Great Plains along the Oregon Trail.

**1854:**
First violent conflict erupts between the Lakota and the U.S. Army.

**1862:**
Gold rush starts in Montana.

**1863:**
John Bozeman and John Jacobs blaze a shortcut to Montana's gold fields through Lakota land in Wyoming.

**1864:**
Colorado militiamen attack a peaceful Cheyenne and Arapaho village along Sand Creek.

**June 1866:**
U.S. troops on their way to open the Bozeman Trail show up at a Fort Laramie peace conference. Red Cloud vows to fight.

**July–December 1866:**
Red Cloud's forces attack soldiers and civilians along the Bozeman Trail.

**December 21, 1866:**
Indians leave no survivors in the Fetterman Fight.

**August 1867:**
Indians fail to break through soldiers' barricades at the Hayfield and Wagon Box fights.

**November 1868:**
After U.S. forces leave the Bozeman Trail, Red Cloud and other chiefs sign the Treaty of Fort Laramie.

**1870:**
Red Cloud takes his first of several diplomatic missions to Washington, D.C.

**1877:**
The United States seizes the Black Hills.

**1909:**
Red Cloud dies December 10 in South Dakota.

**1980:**
The U.S. Supreme Court rules that the Black Hills were taken illegally.

# GLOSSARY

**ambush** (AM-bush)—to attack by surprise from a hidden spot

**decoy** (DEE-koi)—something used to lure a target into a trap

**diplomat** (DI-pluh-mat)—someone who deals with other nations to create or maintain good relationships

**extinct** (ik-STINGKT)—no longer living; an extinct animal is one that has died out, with no more of its kind

**Great Plains** (GRAYT PLANES)—the broad, level land that stretches eastward from the base of the Rocky Mountains for about 400 miles (644 km) in the United States and Canada

**lure** (LOOR)—to tempt someone to do something or go somewhere

**reservation** (rez-er-VAY-shuhn)—an area of land set aside by the government for American Indians; in Canada reservations are called reserves

**sacred** (SAY-krid)—holy

**siege** (SEEJ)—an attack designed to surround a place and cut it off from supplies or help

**skirmish** (SKUR-mish)—a small fight that lasts for a brief time

**strategy** (STRAT-uh-jee)—a careful plan or method

**treaty** (TREE-tee)—an official agreement between two or more groups or countries

# READ MORE

**Collins, Terry.** *Into the West: Causes and Effects of U.S. Westward Expansion.* North Mankato, Minn.: Capstone, 2014.

**McLaughlin, Timothy P., ed.** *Walking on Earth and Touching the Sky: Poetry and Prose by Lakota Youth at Red Cloud Indian School.* New York: Abrams Books for Young Readers, 2012.

**Sanford, William R.** *Oglala Lakota Chief Red Cloud.* Berkeley Heights, N.J.: Enslow, 2013.

**Zimmerman, Dwight Jon.** *Saga of the Sioux: An Adaptation from Dee Brown's Bury My Heart at Wounded Knee.* New York, Henry Holt, 2011.

# INTERNET SITES

FactHound offers a safe, fun way to find Internet sites related to this book. All of the sites on FactHound have been researched by our staff.

Here's all you do:

Visit *www.facthound.com*

Type in this code: 9781491420355

Super-cool stuff! Check out projects, games and lots more at www.capstonekids.com

# CRITICAL THINKING USING THE COMMON CORE

1. Red Cloud didn't have as many guns and other weapons as his enemy, but he had other advantages. Name three. (Key Ideas and Details)

2. The Fetterman Fight was a decisive victory for American Indians. What factors made it so? Is Red Cloud responsible for all of them? If not, who is and why? (Integration of Knowledge and Ideas)

3. The timeline on page 29 is a summary of events. What other details could be included there? (Craft and Structure)

# INDEX

J B REDCLOUD

Higgins, Nadia.
Defending the land

SOF

R4002310736

SOUTH FULTON BRANCH
Atlanta-Fulton Public Library